POEMS BY ANNE WALDMAN

SKIN

MEAT

BONES

Coffee House Press   ::   Minneapolis   ::   1985

Acknowledgments: Some of these poems have appeared in the following publications: *Ballet Review*, *Bombay Gin*, *Friction*, *Mag City*, *Out There*, *The Paris Review*, *The Poetry Project Newsletter*, *Rocky Ledge*, *Tangerine*, *The Vajradhatu Sun*, *The World*, *Tyuonyi*, and *United Artists*.

Special thanks to Lynn Lynn for her unmitigated support all these years.

Cover drawing by Barbara Bash after figure by Senabu Oloyade, Nigeria. Jacket photograph of author by Gerard Malanga.

Copyright © 1985 by Anne Waldman

The Publishers wish to thank the National Endowment for the Arts, a federal agency, for a Small Press Assistance Grant that aided in the production of this book.

Coffee House Press books are available to the trade from Bookpeople, Bookslinger, Publishers Group West, and Small Press Distribution, or they can be ordered directly from the publisher. For catalogs or further information write to:

    Coffee House Press / Box 10870 / Minneapolis, MN 55440

Composition in Weiss by Peregrine Cold Type. Designed by Allan Kornblum. Coffee House Press books are printed on acid-free paper and sewn in signatures to ensure durability.

Library of Congress Cataloging in Publication Data

Waldman, Anne, 1945-
  Skin meat bones.

  I. Title.
PS3573.A4215S5 1985   811'.54   85-21331
ISBN 0-918273-15-3

Contents

7	Queen
8	Skin Meat Bones
12	I Digress...
17	The Lie
18	Dialogue
19	Poor Sport
20	Sidney's Complaynt
21	Far from My Heart
22	Of a Cruel Mistress
23	Gestures in Red
24	Go, Poem
25	Valentines
26	Lullaby
27	Men & Women
29	Hopes & Fears
37	Mammoth
38	Torpedo
39	Berthe Morisot
40	Goddess of Wisdom Whose Substance Is Desire
43	It Sounds It
55	Why I Meditate
56	Why I Meditate
56	Chlor-Trimeton
58	Crack in the World
62	Billy Work Peyote
64	Triolet
65	Allhallows Eve
66	My 16
68	Lethe
69	Canzone
72	Last Dinner
73	Science Times
94	Said So

for my father
John M. Waldman

The living beings are making a noise down below
The living beings make a noise like many different instruments
—A<small>KKANTILELE</small>
(Cuna Indian)

Queen

My sandpaper husband who
wears sackcloth when I don't behave
says Come sit on rattan, woman
Your will is as brittle as glass
Your mad mouth is untamable
& your heart is always in another country

Your ears are radar stalks
Your eyes magnetize yardmen
& when you sing you shake the house
AHHHHH   AHHHHH   AHHHHH
My wife is a burning house

My silky husband who tends the garden
whose arms shake like branches in a storm
complains I'm a slugabed on his time
He says Wake up woman of sleep & cream
Wake up & sweep back your flickering night-lids

Your hands are leopardesses
Your shins are Cadillacs
Your thighs are palaces of tears
When you weep the house rises
My wife is the Indian Ocean rising

My husband of sacred vows
has October weather in his voice
He says Come to bed, amorous woman
Your ancient desk is covered with leaves
Your tardy poem can't be coaxed
But will come to you like a Queen.

skin
        Meat
                BONES   (chant)

I've come to tell you of the things dear to me
& what I've discovered of the skin
                            Meat
                      BONES

your body waking up so sweet to me   skin

dawn light it's green   skin

I'm in hungry repose
                Meat

it's getting close to motion   O skeleton
                                    BONE

you might stretch it now   skin

so warm, flesh

and lasting awhile
              BONE

clock like a BONE creaking
memory like a BONE creaking

little laughter lines around the eyes   skin
& how the mouth's redder than the rest   Meat
or nipples off purple rib cage of
                          BONES

It's morning anywhere!

O sitting and lying around in my weary tinsel skin
got to get up and walk around in my cumbersome skin
put on lightweight cotton skin
& shuffling skin slippers

the light's going to make it raw   skin
or vulnerable   Meat
or hard
        BONES

I could pierce it   skin
I'll grow new skin, undergo big character change

please get under my skin   take hold of me
interest or annoy me intensely

jump me out of my skin!

no skin off your nose, buster
he's thin-skinned, she's thick
dermis & epidermis mating

Allen's nephew once had a skin
                        head
                               haircut

O POOR FLAYED DEER WITH GENTLE HAIR

film on surface of milk this morning

only skin deep

let's go to the oily skin flick

TENDENCY OF HIGH FREQUENCY ALTERNATING CURRENT
TO FLOW THROUGH THE OUTER LAYER ONLY OF A CONDUCTOR

okay, you've wounded me, but it's only skin deep

I'm sitting down in my sweet smelling clammy skin
to eat some juicy MEAT!

one man's meat is another man's poison

animal flesh is tasty

HAD A DREAM THE MEAT WAS TURNED INSIDE OUT,
FLOWERS BLOOMING THERE

Had a dream the jackals came (this was in India)
to collect the Meat of my father's forefingers

O cloud shaped like a tenderloin steak

tree Meat

Meat of Buddha

Had a Meat sandwich   had a Meat day
everyone was carrying their Meat around, flinging
it in the breeze

Small town, downtown, spring: time to show off your Meat
go home when it's dark and sit down with the
                                          BONES

I live in a bare BONES room
he's working my fingers to the BONE
my friend Steven is living close to the BONE
I'm BONING up on my Dante, William Carlos Williams,

Campion and Gertrude Stein

Why is he such a bonehead? won't listen to a thing I say
Why are they so bone idle? won't do a thing I say
I'M GONNA POINT MY ABORIGINE BONE AT YOU & GET YOU WISER!

I've got a BONE to pick with the senator

I've got a BONE to pick with the Pentagon

The BONE of contention has to do with whether or not
we get a lease

Our old '68 Ford's an old BONE-shaker

Ivory, dentine, whalebone, dominoes, dice, castanets, corset
are some of the things made of BONE

but after I die make of my BONES, flutes
and of my skin, drums
I implore you in the name of all female deities wrathful &

                                                                  compassionate

& PROTECT ENDANGERED SPECIES ALSO!

This piece is intended to be read aloud, singing the words "skin," "Meat," "BONES" as notes: "skin," high soprano register; "Meat," tenor; "BONES," basso profundo. The 3 notes may vary, but the different registers should be markedly distinguishable.

I Digress . . .

It's something like the Merode altarpiece by Campin
at the Cloisters. Keep coming back to details.
Foreshadow being & doing in the world. The painting's
gratuitous, abstruse to most modern mortals.
Denaturation of words, fabricate upper panels, call it
cerebral, hermetic, religious, gleeful, laconic, sumptuous
& all the actions are involved in the paint: hatred
& love. I'm through with quarrels of salons, you
know how they were upon me, tear them out of their
semantic field day, throw out the yellow journalists
of bad grammar & terrible manner. Looks all the world
like retinal painting, mellifluous-tongued enigmatic
qualities of objects. What does that little bird symbolize?
Joseph makes mousetraps and bait boxes. Scent of
turpentine on a sweatshirt, rudeness of the dog, baby's
kindness, & a song about not being able to leave a
room. Let's have a good prank & consider it birdlike.
Rearrange the altar, reverse the position of the graven
images. It's a reflected image of you, my good man,
my good woman which is partly concealed & partly revealed.
Who's within? A man-woman made up of 5 agglomerates:
form, feeling, perception, intellect & consciousness.
It's the process of patterns of the evolution of the
world. Something is visible, something is apparent.
I am stuck in a chronology. Down on my knees with
gratitude at the Pergamum in East Berlin for how those
statues were preserved, survived a great war. The
ripples of her stony hair recalled to me the sea or
electromagnetic fields, snakes. Your eyes go mad for
a statue that comes to life. I took a trip on the Wansee
to calm down. Every thought gives off a throw of the dice
(Mallarmé). Lugubrious but also lovely, depicting the
art works as apparatus it all comes to one: the room is

open to the public mind. Learning to behave like a coding
system, I signal you, finger to cheek, to say we must
be going, I left something breathing on the stove ...
Is it the silver or moon condition which has to be raised
to the sun condition? No reply in this quarter of the
mistresses, the dakinis of the east. You don't have to be
inscrutable, just walk around me, observe me. I don't
have a dry mind but enter any painting with clues from
my life. This one holds a bandana, that one a mystical
hook for catching up projections. O Mode of Thought, I
make the rules. For lobby visitings sit quietly. For
hospital visitings walk swiftly through the contaminated
hallways. Have no salient entanglements with the primal
energies at this point. You are beginner's mind swimming
in the labyrinth or hope refracted through a hard glaze,
breaking into the sun condition. O man of the morn, man
of the norm, o mountain man. I would absorb the lessons
you tender, you teach, the lessons of the mathematicians
& alchemists. I finally understand that force is not
mass but also want nothing insoluble here, please. I
have an adept's unfried brain that points to one simple
thing: window dressing. Behind it? Bisexuality has
always been an act of divinity, mercury & sulphur mixing
in the chemistry of the god-goddesses. We have reached
the sky, they said, WE ARE IMMORTAL! Playing *Die Zauberflöte*
on Saturday morning makes the week converge nicely, a
delectation of the beautiful sound that would boom onto
St. Mark's Place or down the canyon from Eldora. It feels
naked to grin like creature of habit: the creature of
pinks & purples, the creature who is papa, the creature
that beats on a crate out my window says he's of Hindu
sect & causes a street argument, the Penitentes of El Rito
with their cookout & bake sale, the anonymous creatures
seeking enlightenment who live on the outer ring of
utopias, working in to the fiery center. You are on a
moving train, you look out the window & see the other

train moving. Can you now explain relativity? Creatures
that surface from the Weather Underground, creatures
that surface for you to be in love with, creature with
hair like cornsilk, creature that desires you be there
feeding, creature that draws a circle in the sand,
creature fixing a stove, taking apart a generator,
flashing the cupola with tin. Time surely doesn't go
in one direction. There is some desire to identify
oneself with conflicts related to the outside world.
Are they internal or external? This is the form part.
Imagine you are building a fortress for your ego. It
likes the padding. But it needs objects of attraction
or repulsion. It needs to make *you* substantial, you
lover, you impossible jinxed family, you money, you
miss preacher, you goody two-shoes. Should I go on?
Then you need to talk about these things in a language
unadorned by personality. It's so difficult. How big
is baby? He's soooooo big. Next, pleasure & pain beyond
physical sensation is the feeling part. Is that form
I see a friend or enemy? I want to reflect off you.
You make me alive, panting for more love, or else
angry about the bath episode. It is a pretense that
there is anything but me here now. The mind/body part
of feeling goes two ways. The mind part is a very
colorful fantasy of how pretty the poem could be, how
luminous that you would wonder at it. No such luck,
but the body part is my relationship to all of you, you
as solid Greg or Katie, something to count on. It is
my version of you I cling to enthusiastically, out
shopping at the Korean vegetable market. Perception is
the third agglomerate and is based on that which is manifested by form and feeling and that which is not. Refer
back to ego headquarters. 25,000 miles to the ends of
the earth. Do you know about the torus, the cloud of
electrified gases circling Saturn that's 300 times hotter
than the sun? Sanskrit for something like intellect

means a tendency to accumulate a collection of mental
states as territory, mental states which are also physical.
There are 51 types of these, some associated with virtue,
some — ignorance, passion, anger, pride, doubt & dogmatism —
associated with its opposite. Then there are bold thoughts,
dogmatic beliefs (eternalism or nihilism) and the neutral
thoughts: sleep or slothfulness, intellectual speculation,
remorse & knowing. You see the point is not to condemn
one kind of thought pattern and accept another even if
it is virtuous. *All* thoughts are questionable. And
they manufacture chain reactions all the time. Like the
echo, your voice bounces back on you as well as being
transmitted to the next wall. Place two
mirrors opposite one another to get a sense of the con-
tinuity and endlessness. Infinite regress. The fifth
is consciousness, which is different from mind. Sanskrit
for mind literally means heart. It's direct & simple,
requiring no brainwork. Consciousness runs behind
living thoughts, it is the kindling for the explicit
thoughts. It is the immediate available source for the
agglomerates to feed on. What we need is a gap with no
kindling twigs. The way of resolving thoughts is through
complete non-evaluation. The agglomerates won't know
what to do because their language is the language of
duality and evaluation. And that's why they keep their
thoughts in a bank! You see how it runs, develops, picks
up steam? I rehearse the speech I am about to deliver.
I notice that I had that thought before, that those wooden
saints on the cloister wall look like big gingerbread
cookies. Creature of old lumps, tender daddies, the
occasion allows a dabbling in rigor, scorn your bravura,
scatter it. Lift your arm. I lift my arm. Lift your
head. I lift my head. Book — this is book. Chair —
this is chair. Calling out to you over the Vermont night,
the New Hampshire night, the Massachusetts night, calling

out to you over the Cherry Valley night, the New York

City night, calling out to you through the California
night, through the Roman night, the Parisian night,
calling out to you over the Afghan night, calling you,
I call you, calling out to you over the Santa Fe night,
the Boulder night, calling out to you over noise of
heavy machines strapped to the boys of the block singing
out some beat I'll go out & get in step with them. I
call out to you like the angel announcing life & death
to Mother Mary & do a little dance to make myself
very small. I do this repeatedly & tell a story
something like the Merode altarpiece painting by
Campin at the Cloisters.

The Lie

Art begins with a lie
    The separation is you plus me plus what we make
        Look into lightbulb, blink, sun's in your eye

I want a rare sky
    vantage point free from misconception
        Art begins with a lie

Nothing to lose, spontaneous rise
    of reflection, paint the picture
        of a lightbulb, or eye the sun

How to fuel the world, then die
    Distance yourself from artfulness
        How? Art begins with a lie

The audience wants to cry
    when the actors are real & passionate
        Look into footlights, then feed back to eye

You fluctuate in an artful body
    You try to imitate the world's glory
        Art begins with a lie
            That's the story, sharp speck in the eye.

Dialogue

Silicon Chip: I know a lot yet do not live
                      My heart's a mockery yet I'll prove strong
                      I have no sex. I serve my masters well
                      Nothing hurts me, I have no prejudice

Clematis: So? I live to hug the pretty house
                All my heads are in the wonderful air
                My mistress loves me
                I am delightful and blue

Silicon Chip: Will you ever perish? Are you wise?
                      Are you never cut down or back?
                      You seem to love yourself
                      Do you have opinions?

Clematis: No and no and no & yet perhaps
                I know I love the sun
                I'm frailer than whoever you are
                & not invented by tenacity
                I sleep when I please & wilt
                & sometimes die

Silicon Chip: Die? Is that to transform & live forever?
                      I've never lived, although I weaken
                      And that's our difference.
                      I am obsolescence
                      Will you flower again?
                      May I call you by name?

Poor Sport

You are an act involving an unintentional deviation from accuracy
You mistake my perception for ignorance as the wingback fumbles
Normal play would have resulted in an out
Or prevented an advance by a masher
You are ignorant of the amplitude
And violate ritual holy water
You have failed in the rackets to return the ball
You made a mistake in court in matters of law or fact
And you have illusions about the nature of reality
Which causes tempers to flare and be obviated
You are a body of false beliefs
In fact to believe is to err and you do that
In artillery fire it's the diversion of a point of impact
From the center of impact in a dispersion of shots:
The distance of a shot from the target
Lapse, faux pas, boner, howler, blunder, bull
You do them all repeatedly approved by imperfection
In the structure of function you are not impeccable
You are deficient and imprudent in your code of behavior
You failed to make a spare
When the previous ball left the split.

Sidney's Complaynt

I think I'm in love & yet complain
Is this love, berated for not loving better?
I think I'm in love but sometimes I wonder
I want pity for being loved, yet get stone cruel
Seeking love, love would be emptier still
Love's hot, am I burned out?
I do what's wrong to get my way beyond desire
I wail for love like I'm poor
Love me, Love me, Love me further!
Love adores itself, it's Cupid's work back & forth
or some dark goddess of perversion
who'd leave you intentionally killed by a kiss
Is it worth it to be smothered alive?
Love, Love, let me be loved, but let me complain.

Far from My Heart

I am carrying this weight around
The dogwood flowering & man is missed
Not just any man, not just any —

To be forlorn
You have to learn to pick your tears up
Drop by drop from the floor

She on the other side is gloating
over nothing
It goes away in the morning

Lover, a vast sadness in your eyes
Tells your silly love of women
Why are you so foolish?

Lush, the bright moon shines on me
I am faithful to you
The sun & the stars

Against my will, hesitating
He comes like the wind
Comes like a shooting star

She is far from my heart
Crosses me so is not my sister

I compete with the sun & moon in brilliance
But with no other woman.

Of a Cruel Mistress

She's cut me out of her life

She strangles the heart of me

My name never crosses her lips

It is a great iniquity

My inward sense doth rage & sorrow alternately

Why does she not mention me with rest of women writing?

Why waste my breath on this fond doting?

Why such perfidy

Why no life of sweet friendship

Why no charity

How welcome would shafts of hate or anger be

It is this nothing that tortures me

I mistrust the words in print I see because they
    excommunicate me

Is this the she I knew, can it be?

She feeds this terrible fire, my unremitting desire.

Gestures in Red

A shadow across my eye. You are memory
You came to me without pause
I loved you. This was certainty

we had. And now more acquainted with destiny
all that belongs to me is in this house
A shadow across my eye. You are memory

and wonder I am spectator. Idly
events came close upon us, struck raw
I loved you terribly. This was certainty

that makes us strangers in the morning certainly
the rocky brow of a hill was
a shadow across my eye. You are memory

I shiver, shadow flickers, my chemistry
rattles in the wind. Events so close once, pass
I loved you terribly. This was certainty

we were betraying ourselves, severity
killed us, passion still gnaws
a shadow across my eye. You are memory
I loved you terribly. This was certainty

Go, Poem

Go, poem, tell him he's
mighty, precise, celebrated
for gesture, motion,
diligence, imagination
in a way makes head
beat, or hearts sting,
brings tears to eye of
stranger & pleasure to
eye of woman

Tell him his mastery as
he bends over, curls under,
supple-spined as cat, airy
as bird, undulant as fish
but with mysterious gaze
of reptile. My poem,
tell him this

A say sometimes it's
sharp October mountain
night ornamented by
stars

Go, poem, to wish him
years of vigor, spirit,
work, of ease in love,
of every reward, renown,
& sharp perception of
his transitoriness &
may I live to see him
live in this & be a
friend for life

Go, poem, tell him I link
his heart in mine tonight.

Valentines

I will write it out: A parable makes
real pictures & colors
on winged feet. She's got patches
on a red rug, pink candles wane
that a Valentine contains lines
which isn't the point but they're nice.
I always loved it's a mother to a
sentimental love. Under "sentimental"
think: understandable. All this is
ledgy now, "sub rhythms" Allen says
You have a rose in you it's mystical
Both have shoes, Poverty not, but the yoke
so gushy on the page, funny after
wheel rage, truck door slam.

Valentine was a martyr I think
sweet accomplishment & suave.
I love we see them present & then
an eclipse of the polished sun.
I would like the heart to suggest a Polish
joke when father's not happy she
paints wedlock. Stiff drinks
toast your honest blue eyes &
shirt with a rose stripe.
In a thin foil of armor, vulnerable
has a way of expanding the moment.
Keep seeing a blimp or feel like
a wanderer. The orchestra
is designing the ideal poetry.

Lullaby

Kind fire   Kind coal
Kind mother so high
All is life
With night's weight

Kind rose   Kind milk
Kind floor so shiny
All's well under the ceiling
All comes true kindly.

Men & Women

A woman goes away thinking the world
remains a frontier: imperishable, vegetal
Correct this. Correct the woman
rather than she be restricted again & again
piercing her retinas with rushing prisms of light

Life is more or less a voyage in light
walking over such questions rough-shod
But the woman comes back as delicate
as any clue. She senses all these random sleeps
pulls up the cover, goes back to sleep

Men refuse to open themselves up
unprepossessing however, if not lightheaded
At times instincts are perverted to hieroglyphs
meaning "I stand in the name of going home"
Myopic scrutiny abounds in "home"
while all component entities revert to

The woman again: effect of sunlight, pastry,
winter cloisterings, insatiable child,
augment this thesis, carrying-on-time-of-month
& being much kinder to crazy people
or becoming an intermediary in realm of art

Men move toward every passing fancy
Women are fixed in a constellation of forms
Some humans find war exciting as world systems pass
& stars are born & die figuring into
the molecules of menacing mankind

Women in whose molecules demonically insistent
life hammers away, you mercilessly
fling yourselves at the heavens as
centers of attention! You men take a whipping
as human counterparts in battle scenes,
grinning skeletons for any eye: Give it up!

Caprice is not a solemn oath swimming
up to the canvas but a more rigorous color
Like a surprising response from the middle of nowhere
Men have different colors too at the end of the chase

Don't try to pull the saint on the energies that be,
although paintings are holy labyrinths too
yet more solid than you'll ever be
marveling at our little men & women sexes & brains
The wind percolates when lovers stop squirming.

Hopes & Fears

Hope & fear hopes & fears
you have them
you had them, hopes & fears you have them

You had them, hopes
You have them, fears
hopes or fears you had them
you have them
hopes & fears you have them

I won't say no, you have them
I will say it plainly you had them
I had them, hopes & fears I have them

Wake in the morning: fear, the clock, the day, I had it
Wake in the afternoon: fear, the clock, quiet, I had it
Fear: the night, noise, the street, I have it
Person beating his body against a building, I saw it
Fear: he had it
She has it
Hopes & fears you have them
All the bodies in morning light: they have it
Wake in the morning: fear, the clock, the day, job,
another person was there, he had it
Wake in the afternoon, she was gone, he had it
Two men: one had it
Two other men: both had it, fear they have it
Two women had fear of being alone
She won't walk down the street alone or say goodbye
Then her friend needed to be talking constantly
They had it
Hopes were had by all for good weather to go apple-picking
Fear: the radio, the forecast, the debt, the man had it

Fear you might get hurt: back off, start again, go home
I have them, hopes & fears I have them
Hope to be safe, fear to be sick, injured, isolated
Hope to be in a well-heated place, a place with light,
another person in the room, I want to know her
I want you: hopes & fears, I want you
I don't have you but I have hope
Fear you will quit my sight
Fear you'll no more be present in my world
I don't have you but I have fear
Fear: I have it
Do you? Do you have it?
Fear: what is it? Fear: who is it?
It isn't you it may be fear
Fear: I'm not here when I should be her
Wake in the afternoon: the clock the telephone the doorbell
Who is it?
Who are they
Are they fixing something up there?
Someone said a name, sounded like Anister Honorful
Raining on the roof: fear

I whispered her name as if to say fear
But I whispered the long way
& she said, because she was close Yes
Yes, she wouldn't have it
She won't have any of it, fear
The summer solstice a day like no other I have it
I had it then, yes
No it won't happen again, fear like that
Fear we had it
I hope to see you & then I hope to see you or
be seen by you in the room of wonderful paintings
I painted myself this way out of fear
Presentable hope in the night, I went out often
I went out hoping to see something reminding me of you

Yes, I had it and it was distinct. It was a thin hope
Someone was an outsider but I knew the name & he
shouted my name to scare me to say I know you I won't be afraid
Outsider on the roof a week ago looking, he said, for a key
Are you succeeding in finding a home you look rich all right
You look rich out of fear
Hoping to be seen outside all of her attitudes
Fear to be taken apart with verbs & nouns & adjectives
Fearing to miss one event never to be repeated again
Could that be
Dare we say that
Hope he survives like the others
I read about the MX missile
It was designed to make you fierce & hopeful
but listen, are you listening   it scares us
I said it is of fear made & fear born like the
monster it is always being Everyone is saying this
over & over out of fear & hope to change the mind, the plan
the instrument of this terrible darkness
It is that simple fear again to be hope
I hope so
I certainly hope so
I meant rich in the sense of complete, not hungry
Fear eats her
We are hoping for a change in the mood
The climate is too hot for right now
I fear it isn't natural to be cooling the drinks like this
Come out from the hot sun
Fears & hopes in the little businesses
The results are promising
I had hoped to visit all the watering spots
I stopped in Brugge because I had a vision
Memling was there to paint us in our car
Was it fear?
He said we had a kind of haunted look
He wore a big Arnolfini hat but I played the bridegroom

A car is scaring the people from another century
I said it won't do not to be polite
Nothing to do with hope or fear
But I always had them both before I wrote
in this great curriculum
a prescription of hope
I watched myself grow fangs in the moonlight
I jumped back at myself
Later I turned fish to get away quick
I had them, you see of course how deceptive it is
Why have fear, why have it?
Not a lot of sense to kill the Tamil people
Sri Lanka a name you could love
The names are instruments of doom
Collectively speaking for fear for hate as in
I hate you world I kill you too
You know this
I was thinking you know this why sing about it?
Hopes & fears you have them
Hopes & fears you had them
You always had them
I won't tell you what you are
Don't tell me or don't you dare
You will be sorry to be a messenger of this
sad news if you accept this, did you ever have them?
I asked Did you do you have them, hopes & fears?
Who is metamorphosing
I want to entertain you with a rendition of something
approximating these words
Look at my eyes!
Hopes & fears, I have them
I had them
Hopes, I had them
I had fear
Hoping to cajole you into neither
I won't have it if I can't have them

Her fear is sweet to her
You sleep as this is forced on you
How can you do this
Wakening among the uncomfortable because as you see
they won't last, the root of it, fear
& hope to live forever
You are the audience of all my hopes & fears
Listen to my hopeful voice now
Inflections say this with all their might
It is in how it is being said
I told you so it was certainly not very hopeful
Fear you will shut down the amplification
before you hear about the torture of many brave
men & women
Can you imagine this?
It happens all the time
Here could be mentioned dioxin
Here is the introduction of poison
It is flourishing but will not flower
Fear: the wind will blow my topcoat off
Cambodia, can you see it?
Can you feel the fear
Hope to be out of it soon
Hope to squirm out of it
This love is one-sided, goodbye hope
She settles down & fears fear like armor
Look at our little sister fear
It was like this
Fear: the others, the school, a voice, I had it
If you have nothing you have fear
It comes out in writing
But this was prescribed to be because you had this busy
mind one day
One day it attributed itself to you
Fear likes you being mad
And fear will make you careful

But I meant to put something back
in about fear before it got so built up
You can't say that about fear she is cunning
Little Renard is afraid of the storm & hides
I watched the singers playing Dido & Aeneas
until they became sublime & went beyond
that to fear
Fear to leave, to be apart, the hero must go on to battle
An empire is forming you can't turn history around
until now
He never left & aged in her arms weak in his fear
The goddesses mock us, hope & fear
So what?
Hopes & fears we have them
Do you have it? Fear?
I suppose so
Certainly so
Yes, I have it. The day, the clock, the voice, doorbell
Cradle me in the boundary of your plan
so the limbs won't break
Break down this hope, this automatic machine
Reflex to hope
Fear in the reflection
I watched myself in the water sprout roots and blossoms
Hope to be there when the time comes
It'll just roll around you'll see
It'll just be there I tell you so
Certainly
I write this as part of the curriculum
Crank up my fears to make them go away
I see you in the rain, I see you widening
I see the big raincoat
I was waiting for you to return
Earlier I had hopes, later I had fears
Hopes & fears I have them, I had them
It went like this: the day, the equidistance, two people

went apart, a noise on the roof, I honored the dead
then a storm, I spoke on the telephone, drug addict?
A witness to lunch, the little dog hid
But it could be even more mundane: clock, money
I want to be hopeful so you get better
Fear won't heal anybody's heart
Turn it around: her fear is sweet to her
What does the Congressman say
Convey her fear to him
Run for cover or stand up with the Quaker
Fear: the dogtag
My fear was her boat, her hope, and let it come out —
her ambition
It launches her it makes her wise
But let it be seen not to be such good advice
to be a victim of her whim and wonder
She would wait for fear if she had to
She would stalk fear
It is the ally of the practice of dying into life
This is strange talk
Writing is a way of canceling them out but
display the colors too
It could be pretty: fear, or fiery at least
Yes with a dress with accouterments
I like the panic that hangs about the window
St. Mark's Place
His sex because he was older (she was a child)
scared her, fear of something you've never seen before
But another one said this never scared her
so she was always secure
Fear you will bite my head off
How I wished to see her face but that was the one part
she would not reveal
He has big paranoid ears
What are they saying about me
A pointed demon, a table of jumping objects, moonless time,

someone calls you out of sleep
Dream my mother was ferrying me to the afterlife in
a gondola through a subway tunnel
Fear I would fall over into the murky depths, underbelly New York
Fear: never see light
Fear: all my hair is chopped off, you don't recognize me
Fear: laughter from the mouths & bellies of vicious animals
Phantoms of a skittish head
I was created in a test tube
The train halted in the middle of Bulgaria, rude officials
demanded papers in an obscure language and took money
Fearful of prison: Iran
They exit with your passports behind curtains, doors, partitions
Cold eyes
My hope goads me on to further raptures
To win the sestina contest!
Let them come to some agreement, everyone suffers
Wake at night: someone going through the bags
Wake at dawn: perfunctory cold & hunger
Old bogeyman Totalitarianism
Fear: life under the gun
Hopes & fears hopes & fears you have them
you had them you have them still
Hopes & fears you have them
Hope to see all the spectacles
Fear I misplaced them
Fear I missed them
jockeying for favor with one more powerful
Traveling by airplane I had them
Traveling in the blue sky I had them
All the precautions make you have them
You are the audience of all my hopes & fears.

Mammoth

Bewilderment acquiescing in a view, my long term to see you
all a bit better, your male retinas. Incongruous, a wheedling
voice in a manly body, discordant results. It's the motion
of a pen against a starchy shirt you can't avoid, you won't
get the best of. This time memories are not grumbling to be
considered. This time, a not-too-territorial room, sitting
down on a theme as if it were a rug. Never so happy as among
these precipices, taciturn you might say, or pleased. No
recriminations. Your predilections match theirs. Wit,
chosen green taffeta, all the sensations of a long sea voyage.
Not tedium as in some snug retreat because we never know
what will happen next. Impressions of brittle attire,
exquisite refinement wasn't ours. We set to work coming out
of our reveries. This time: furious imprecations. This time:
passion. This time: speechless, contemporary of the mammoth,
we remove the imprint of everything not ours.

Torpedo

All hands grow excited

making contact with Bismarck

Steering north won't, maybe, yes, do

Got a chance to intend to attack —

Attack!

Divers down now. Now, *go*!

"Impossible to feel the rudder, sir"

Thinking about the men,

according to custom from holy chaos

So stand I these when weather's good for war.

Berthe Morisot

Toward the end of her life she said that the
wish for fame after death seemed to her an
inordinate ambition. "Mine," she added,
"is limited to the desire to set down
something as it passes, oh, something, the
least of things!"

A critic had written of the show at the
Salon des Impressionnistes singling out
Morisot: "There are five or six lunatics,
one of them a woman."

Goddess of Wisdom Whose Substance Is Desire

for Joanne Kyger

You want distraction's collar & necktie
She is something embracing a human document
but I fear you'll never twice spy land
modulating boredom & fatigue
with fashionable closet people
whose spasms of prudent laughter
are acute in your wake — No!
Won't do for you.

But she: gracious pleats, fits,
who owns all graces, slips, who is
no matinee twit, is a beam, who won't fall,
a supple frank movement, is a gracile planet
to know, circled by fixed heat,
benign of big eyes, obscure of sternness,
bears no ill labels, a pinafore hopping
on a leg, is mature of reason, who has a
sound reason, is a veritable pouch
of information, a saint

Also a bunch of winter traces,
glistening clips, is a clipper,
a bold one, a maiden to film
to smile to clasp to form your thoughts,
loath to make a plea of axis of world
shifting, mind's discreet parody of self,
slave to livingroom harmony, mine gates
are reluctant attitudes compared to hers,
profiles in wood to make a pleasure
quarter hum in pleasure garter to make
pleasure rather a saint too, she's got
a strange cook's manner for handling limbs

> *When women make concessions*
> *who dares not dumbly bend*
> *who dares not humble bread*
> *or stumble up a cliff for it*
> *to fondle her head . . .*

Renunciation is sweet to her
checking out packages with a shiny face,
journeying without escort, without
a married name, wearing the cut cloth
of nourishment, traveling incognito's
seamy route of transport, dispel hot
tantrum, gum braids, triumphant
over gleaming mail, not in sense of manly
but mail of metal made
& substance of desire made woman

She feeds on rapscallion envy of this age
merriment & poverty smiling there
corpses, vultures, idiot grinning there,
impatience too, & ghosts smiling there
& lesser hells of deceit of many moons
& many mistakes there
& there — a tiredness, there — a charm
to fuck against bleakness, there —
accomplished treachery
there's no wink, gone slack
dizzy or stupid or vexed

No paths apart to croak a fiction
to make an evil faction of this dire want
or wrath falling or plowing proudly
decked out like a male bird of the species

> *wolf music: come here tonight*
> *arguments: go to the podium*
> *owl song: friend indeed*
> *mermaid: smooth a lash*

Or lash against her pagan power
she whose substance, whose wisdom is desire
whose slaughter echoes laughter and earbone hisses
she who appointed herself to your distraction
she whose wish is in the light

A modest stipend, she is no mother diminishing,
her dreams are ornaments of sleep
She's a sharp retina of perception
when you stray, when you are too peppery,
when you are not your blunt self
when you are a foil, a bitch
shrinking up like this itinerary's list
to arrive musically at rest
not a stag, not a suitor in jealous weeds
but optimistic & boosting speech.

It Sounds It

You & I out of all dreaming:

Of this you are understood, of measurement, of predicament.
I fear I do not exist we'll not exist you give a candidate
such a time, predicated on false belief. Over a small town's
cab radio: Pick up Stevie Wonder at Harvest House. Not a
blink or raised lash but static of reserve. Now pick up
Eldridge Cleaver who is "passionately against Welfare."
Make a remark: Time, how strange you are to us. Make your
mark, the European would say, free of the wild weed of delusion.
We are all after all all of us as often as not on the mark.
On the money. Freeze these assets and markedly lethal weapons.
Of course you may curse what has been done to you Dear Member
Of the Senate. Dear Warrior Woman of Blatant Dimension: the
space inside equals theoretic bedtime story. She is a princess,
of course, that some flesh-tone touch-tone Princess, the same
American stammerings calling after a Yellow Cab. If I ask
for a pen he thinks I'm going to a fare check or check this
wondering myself at many things, dollars. Of course not a
whole city went & sealed this occasion in anyone's favor
at a primary in any cabbie's mirror. Lauper at C.U., Jackson
in Denver & all the daughters went & sealed this occasion.
The seal & mark of any fair time is what you're doing, what
I'm, in any moment renouncing any influence from him, her,
it, them in medias res, restless & absorbed all about moving,
to move or be moved went the time the tide went the good
nature went as mute as any comment or seal with a western
kiss. He's taken the measure in a prodigious glare, something
said much greater than it sounds ...

A slow mind served the candidate well, the mark of any animal,
petted down, below the chair. Ah, the dog can't vote.

I mark the ballot like a good citizen. I can make a cross
like anyone ought to be able to but is it a delusive LAST DAY
to register October 5th? Went the Harvest time, all fall
down. Did Wonder vote? Will Cindy bop or Black Elk speak?
Moved west, went the theocratic resolve using language to say
something that's never been said: like: What is mirrored in
language I can't use. But agreeing nonetheless with she, I,
they, the consolation nearest her with genius in his eye (not
the senator) but a scenario: She had a female lover they got
married & got her brother to donate sperm so she, the other,
could have the baby but then they broke up & she wants
Visiting Rights, her brother's child, she's nothing but a
doting aunt. But what would the Platform say to this? Is
it perverse in Dorn's sense as "against the family"? I'm
waiting on a great moment, pulling the lever all welcome all
the new citizens who always glide off with smoothness to
another subject. The political nightmare the mark of the
lesbian, the concomitant, the looser ones, coming unhinged
in an impious way, like the student who falls off his chair
when I read Olson aloud, he flaps wings, his arms are a
wheel or whorl, where are we going in anyone's lurid imagination?
Names who are the repository for anybody to touch. You
touch me, touch me, don't bristle. The cat assaults the
image, a virtuous act to be not so expectant, as a child
says "exposed to," he's supposed to not never know nothing
better. An authoritarian voice provides all the
corrections wanting to rip the "reals" out of their mouths:
real good, real nice, real smart, real never speaking to me,
real silence, real prompt, real enough of what I know, real
strong, real quick lift to the issue, backbone, femur. To
say all that before counting on me: real pressure, real death,
real everything almost with the smile of a child, real
Nicaragua, no slate can hold the figures as he makes them
stand at attention, tiny soldiers & villains in space. The
space is my villain, he says, rocked back into bed, & you
are my only mother: real sky, real scarce, how long do you

give me, real obvious ploy, real temperament, real terror,
real turf, clean-cut walkways, real sweet, real animals,
genuine food.

I'll stand again as if in trance under Jupiter for the passage
of middle years, witness the cast of any vote. Like the priest
Mayans they would pick a low energy day, no full or beginning
moon, no ground swell, a waning situation so the activists
stay home. Come out of your delicate rooms into the discreet
booths of fixed chance. A ruse or result, a resumed situation,
a sense of subtle wantonness, what is at stake. Irritation,
damnation, poverty, cruelty, neglect, real easy, but if I
thought what you thought or if whoever you are thought whatever
she could never figure out, or if they all went, acknowledged,
acclaimed the Tibetan doctor's advice to one young son that
he not watch scary movies or moves, the ... Eyes move over the
intensely white linen, the semigloss off-white walls, a
rattan sofa, the newly waxed floor, the front door with a
Christian symbol marked in metal, a, emblem, a, place, an,
incision, a, how in the world you've done it, a world, or
how in the world your vitals scared at your own heroism an
act of violence. A signet, a peace treaty, the depiction of
a Buddhist deity with eyes in her hands, feet. Eyes everywhere,
totally awake.

WAKE UP

Every single proposition can be brought to a particular form
in this case a wild shout

MAKE IT UP

You the proxy, you the volunteer
or cast a VOTE, A SHADOW, A FIRST STONE

as a signal to begin counting. The loser concedes winning
is the order of the day, a command, the eyes shut down real
fast predicting rain

Also, there was a bay horse for me to ride, as in my vision

2

Begun to throb, their human questions
comparison with other life forms:
urgent to communicate with his lips
become more interesting or what has kept you?
a jewel brilliant & hard
what has kept you
a tree with a bird in it, a holiday
what has kept you
a nightmare, a frightening cleaver
what has kept you
a book making sense, a robber in the street,
one gooseneck lamp
what has kept you
an illogical situation, a job to do
my own lassitude, am I late?
Am I to punctuate this mark
like a small prayer
forever supining
supplicating
forever obscuring, like a tall Sally
like a long tall Sally, like Sally's ride
what comes next?
So I won't play you that trick
In a long tall column
I won't put my mark here
what did I do
I'm all shook up, garbled a sentence
lost the small battery
found the neighborhood
changed, what did I do?
scarce knew what:
run, walk, speak, wonder
speak, sing, vo-code
every last syllable

her expression had of being most natural
eyes fixed as of a mute statue
heart of bronze
what happened?
a wedding, a death, one small story
the death of a small store
what happens?
A tremendous bristling explosion
the air of that amplitude is now doubtless strange
It sounds strange to me
It sounds like stepping back into a room
where I wasn't ready to go out there yet

MX Trident Minuteman Poseidon
too thick for going out there yet
not a matter in dispute
what happened?
but a stockpiling
what happens?
the leaders speak as if under water
mesmerized by a mythical deterrent
abhorrent detergent
what? What happens?
we look for the detriment or a measure
of the possible wretchedness
You are not a space treaty in my dream
but villains in space

I, I, and I, & yet again I
& you are you are you are you yet again
you
out of all dreaming

I or I or I or you but you but you
out of all dreaming

I say what you think or think I say what
you think
do I?
You think I'm thinking like you
am I?
you think you can say it?
Can we agree on any of the issues?

in the light, I am not at all dreaming
in the light of this predicament
blatant dimensions, the situation continues
out of hand

hand it over
or handle with care
welfare

A man of public office
entered the party for the Nicaraguan delegates
at whose instigation?
with a cane
Cyclops?
Spiderman?
Hidden behind brute eyes
invoke a terrible time
of espionage
Return to a vatic voice
O help us Medicine Buddha
"grassroots" inroads
Jalapa, your torn spirit
bounces back
in the fortitude
of one Selfida Hernandez
Her gaze is steady:
what eyes have seen
where she's been

Torture
out of all dreaming
the old game:
who's doing it to whom
murder at the Honduras border
she & her dead son out of all dreaming
muscles out of all being
this weakened white person
sits at the top of the food chain
write or try to witness
try to get behind her eyes *en español*

por favor

mi amiga
esperanza

Understood back of human questions
a throb
murmur of the huge collective life
putting forth not exactly perfections
as the candidate rouses a smile
musters the old geography
looks haggard
but comes to life on any issue
would renunciation provide a moral glamor?
give up the inbred suspicion
hand o'er the privy purse
a long career behind him,
ardently over the finished meal
the ruse, the counterintelligence
the samurai in me wants to engage
your attention for a long time
as long as it takes
to win the man

the moral fiber
behind the eyes
rods & cones in my
preternatural laboratory of stimulation
not losing game or battle
it sounds like the first part of
a symphony

announce my theme & come on in
make the place your own

it sounds
it comes to me
The creation story told by Tibetan doctor
how semen mixed with moisture on a leaf
it made a woman outta me
she bops & all the daughters went & sealed this occasion
& the goddess of poetry Sarasvati shook her body
& strummed her vina
the plants stopped fussing
any hairdo you want for sale on any mall
her locks coiled in spirals of sound
nothing costs dollars
in the light of
acute & deliberate action
I mean you can't get anything done for that
at the Target store
I was aiming to get there
on a blind date

3

Newton showed that for every action there
is an equal & opposite reaction. This
holds true for the arms race as it does
in physics

"Anything you undertake is based on outlook"

a 17-year-old friend's
point of
character
is on a line
how to be
a good one
want
the world
to think
well
of him

I remember, too,
lying to save my grace

little Lego towers
the 4 directions
& arms like ram's horns
remind me of
upheavals
on a Zapotec rug
accidents in the wool

clear sentences he said he wanted
blasting Carla

it sounds like my last mistress
it sounds like my mistress's eyebrow
it sounds like a 25-gallon acid spill

Syntax technicians rushed to the scene, fire personnel
put a temporary seal on the ruptured fitting, & soda ash
on the spill to neutralize the hydrochloric acid
Vulcan spokespersons could not be reached for comment

What you say is what you are
You might be a naked booby star

It sounds like what you meant to be saying

It sounds like they memorized their debate
You were saying something?
It sounds all wasted & thou hast hands
thou hast ears thou shalt die of a thousand thous
It sounds, & yet to be understood

It sounded like a good idea

It sounds of darkness, day gone
An ancient scar upon this picture
It sounds like much to this man or woman is due
It sounds: my heart doth bind
It sounds not a lot like stagecraft

Words remain in memory
their essential simplicity & strength
like open air & fresh water elements

He hath learned a trick from Flavio
It sounds hot on the tongue but later
it's cool, or rather it sounds cold
A creature remains in the room
although you know
I don't think we were created at all
as well as try to find out any's thoughts
& tread the sun & be more bright than he
I thought it sounded a bit obscure
keep the obsequies in mind, the decline
of a noble ignoble arms race

4

Where does it gather
or gathered it not here, potable & compendious

Of this you aren't stood for or stood up to because you are
the president. Do you know him the child asks and what
is he? is he a man? a voice? a radio? what is it or rather
no one would ever want to do that in another dimension like
Teddy Roosevelt. Would you? Would Groucho Marx? So much
faith on either part but knowing the facts or having depth
or dice. No dice but it could represent a lost ballot.
No mercy will burn the coals, stroking the pleasure of
poetry with the pleasure of politics or of other puzzles,
you name any kind of respite needed here:

HELP

Jeane Kirkpatrick says we all knew Brutus was an honorable
man whose poems passed from hand to mouth in manuscript
before the onslaught of these waves

it sounds like rubbish to me
or irresponsible, meaning the same
it sounds pugilistic & strange
"to the stars through difficulties"
or something like that
something said that was supposed to be
naming your own fate, to say it slant
slant-out, politician-like
What are you driving at?
You, out of all dreaming
but to those of us who unkindly were
scattering to shine it makes no sense

Petty thoughts go off
it sounds rather like a wonderful place

to go off to but
it sounds fishy
the people are bewildered
the people are inebriated
by the magnificence of the scene

To be a little wilderness
Who would guess?
to be so coy
or compare a great thing with a small one

& out of all dreaming,

this scheme

Why I Meditate
A reply for Allen Ginsberg

I sit because I'm wing'd with awe
I sit because the poetry scene got sour in America in 1980
I sit because Milarepa did
I sit because Padmasambhava buried the Bardo Thotrol in the
    Gampo Hills & gave endless transmission to discover how death
    is liberating
I sit because Yeshe Tsogyal appeared in a dream & showed me
    her cervix like an ocean
I sit because the Dakinis dance over my forehead
I sit because thoughts chase thoughts
I sit in Puri they won't let me in the Hindu temple
I sit in Bodnath under the 8 eyes of the great stupa
I sit in Calcutta like being in Preta realm
I prostrate 1,000 times under the descendant of Buddha's
    bodhi tree
I sit like a frog on Cherry Valley's poetry farm
I sit by her hospital door, breathe in my mother's eyeball
    pain
I sit like an agent provocateur on the Orient Express
I sit like a cow in farmer Lang's meadow
I sit inside the body of a nursing mother
I sit to scandalize
I sit because I won't take it lying down
I sit to test old friends & loves
I sit because passion burns me up
I sit because I'm a paranoid speed freak
I sit because I deserted the poetry wars
I sit to be exile from Ego's land.

Chlor-Trimeton

Restore to battle under the sun: Chlor-Trimeton. Restore to
battle pollen under the sun. In place of battle use mettle,
in place of your sun another one. Restore to all galaxies
an escape from allergies for who but us here, earth dwellers,
can escape lest we be carved in obsidian in caves twenty times
darker than darkest night where nothing enters in, airtight
in dwindling air, but not despair to be so fixed, inhuman.
Restore to battle my defenses: Chlor-Trimeton. What Ever You Are
you make me sneeze, no you make me light up, no you make sense
of words I write in fit upon me, June, Chlor-Trimeton. Trim my
tons. Pantothenic acid discovers calcium in the night in bone
marrow, let's go there. Narrow it to one substance, one antidote.
Let's go in there, the narrows in the Cave of Chlor.

We left home, a family of travelers: a baby boy, a teenage god-
daughter with eyelashes & creams & theories all in a ton truck.
I woke in the country in a tree of styrofoam, there was someone
peeking in the bird-hole. Then an old lady placed a non-allergenic
bouquet at my feet to signal my womanhood. She was like a human
bundle in a whirl of dust. You are now the moth, she said. We had
left the city, hard shell, and left behind, hard sell. Why should
I be resisting to be a vessel for medicine in this wide world?

We want to see the bugs walking around the children say, there are
so many of them but we won't kill them we just blow them away.
Stinging eye to be such pain such outdoors where you are biggest ego-
sneezing-thing around. Restore to battle stations: Chlor-Trimeton.
The Haitians arriving in all conditions of reaction & disease. In
Sanskrit such a thing might not exist. Resistance is built in but
nations inflict a battle & everyone keep their station to be so
fixed, inhuman. Take my reactions away. I can't go on without
these cures, these lures, these wars to be embalmed free of itch
of sting, sing again Chlor-Trimeton.

I'll read to you about the patty pan and the confusion of pies &
2 animals having golden tea in a story. The exhausted storybook
animals are restored to battle with camomile tea, sometimes to
be an eyewash too, a salve for rubbing and calm the nerves, the
paws, not to be confused with store-bought remedies, false-face
enemies of immune systems, sing: put away Chlor-Trimeton.

I want to ride well aware away from nuclear detonations in silver
truck with totem boy and totem pubescent daughter and Authority
will drive. To what do I owe this reaction, this way of sounding
of breathing of seeing? For when you sneeze it is said the moon
receives a little more of your energy & you are made simpler in mind.

I sneezed my mind away on this summer day year 1983 in the hills of
Cherry Valley, bypassed by the Erie Canal, home of poets & dreamers
& children & sugar & starch. If I could stop rubbing my eyes I would
probably see the world as it really is.

Crack in the World

I see the crack in the world

My body thinks it, sees the gaping crack in the world

My body does it for me to see

Blood flowing through the body crack

Body, send your rivers to the moon

Body twists me to the source of the moon

It turns me under a wave

It sets up the structure to make a baby, then tears it down again

Architecture of womb-body haunting me

Someone is always watching the ancient flow

It doubles up my mind

Ovum not fertilized

I see the crack in the world

Thoughts intersect in the body

He must not keep me down

Let me go my way alone tonight

No man to touch me

A slash in me, I see the slash in the world tonight

It keeps me whole, but divides me now

Out on land, to bleed

Out on street, to bleed

In the snow, blood

This is a South American song

Scent of oleander

Or this is a cactus song

Sing of a blood flower a rose in the crotch

O collapsible legs!

My body enchanted me to this

My body demented to this

It is endometrium shedding

I am compressed in the pressure of my heart

It is life pursuing the crack in the world

Between worlds

Between thoughts

A vacant breath

Words won't do it

Ovum not fertilized

The man hasn't done it

I cover every contingency
the catty one
or puritan walking in a fecund world

Words sing to me of endometrium collapse

Words go down to my belly

Back swelling, to put my body next to the earth

This is periodic

It comes at the full moon

Let me go howling in the night

No man to touch me

Don't fathom my heart tonight, man

No one wants to be around this factory,
this beautiful machine
but I shun your company anyway

My flexible body imagines the crack

Body with winds

See the crack in the universe

The curse, glorious curse is upon me

Don't come to my house

Don't expect me at your door

I'm in my celibacy rags

My anthropocentric heart says there's
a crack in the world tonight

It's a long woman's body

It's a break in the cycle of birth & death

It's the rapid proliferation of cells
building up to die

I make up the world & kill it again & again

I offer my entrails to the moon

Ovum not fertilized

Architecture haunting me

Collapsible legs you must carry the world

You get away from me

You keep your distance

I will overpower you with my scent
of life & death

You who came through the crack in my world

You men who came out of me, back off

Words come out of the belly

Groaning as the world is pulled apart

Body enchanted to this

Body elaborated on this

Body took the measure of the woman
to explain the fierceness of this time
walking on the periphery of the world.

Billy Work Peyote

*A piece of sympathetic magic
for the life of William Burroughs, Jr.
(died March 3, 1981)*

Keep it moving, Billy. There's some motion. We're doing the clog
dance for ya, embattled or exalted   Motions of fronds.

    These support systems   these rivers falling in & through you
you way back deep deep deep legroom not enough to sit down & whisper
in your ear Billy   no nova Billy   More nourishment
    Billy we send you these stars dotted on the dotted swiss
a most delicious gray for the senses   here Billy take them Billy
take these stars Billy   here Billy take the woodsmoke
        (moving Billy moving Billy moving keep it moving)

We send you these scents & the pleasure of making a tent
    a tent for wanderers for a wandering soul   lost your shadow
here's a body to come back to Billy
        & for your sake we lie down
in a bundle of cloud & for you we eat this medicine to cure
    & puke it up again   I vomited for you Billy & the last
3 years come back up to me for you Billy   churn it around
You are still here for us Billy
        we three   me   Steven   Reed
in still night I can't sit still jumping up for you Billy
    moving keep moving keep it moving Bill
        corn liquor to get the magic down

demodulation Billy

demon hypodermic Billy

                corrigible Billy

Solomon's seal Billy

it's wobbling Billy

correlation Billy

           stock still

                indelible

    hyacinth blood Billy

       cards on the table Billy

          high drama & we're missing you Billy

      Where ya been Billy boy

looking for you Billy

   studying your shank Billy
     universality Billy
          let it go
              passing it around

moving keep it moving Billy moving keep it moving Billy moving
    keep it moving Billy Billy moving keep it moving Billy
        moving keep it moving Billy moving keep it Bill

Triolet

A perfectly clear liquid like water
flows out of the spine

Last night in the hospital, this is what I saw

I don't know where this fluid sits
& what its design

A perfectly clear liquid like water
flows from her spine

Does it move from the brain in a line?

The cool doctor draws it out with a straw

A perfectly clear liquid like water
flows out of the spine

Last night, in the cold hospital, this is what I saw.

Allhallows Eve

My mother's
ghost
is up
in me
as I sit
on trolley bus
hand on
chin
resigned
to the
passing
world
as she was
always,
thinking
it
so.

My 16

Combat, as thing of highest importance
    Raillery & love, she was a humanist
        Reader's full bloom, O she was my love

Our etiquette not worse than any person's
    family. Weep tears, go to your room
        & be a captured cow. Be in your body
            prison, girl. What is this magic?

Tits swell, no peace now, and such
    a dance in our small rooms, to cradle
        the telephone, it was a blond

Erotic element, sublime distemper, checking
    for drugs in eyes, mouth, pocket. Plenty
        interference all the way, she's on tail
            down Macdougal to Fat Black Pussy Cat cafe

Caught drinking brandies in Punjab
    hatchecking on sly underage for quarters
        I had some secret lovers

Hurt to be known but hurt not stable
    equilibrium. A fit she had, me too
        I thought we'd part, no that's not the sport
        not rules, not dream we assume

No annihilation of this the relationship
    of whole life. We're linked
        I'd glorious mother her

She'd quake under disapproval
    But you're so moral that's the trouble
        Don't you know things exist double
            like I could be this, and this too, Mother?

How can you! she'd cry, it's risk for a woman
    Caution, beware. Screaming I'd protest
        I'm just human

            No, no, not that — Never —
            You're mine — my angel — my one —
            Precious darling daughter:
            Don't kill my heart!

Lethe

after H.D.

Nor child painted sick
nor other rocking motion
nor love's cool anger in pretty room
nor woman's lonely station
nor cold winter
maturest fears
button up! button up!
nor New York City's toys
Nor Edwin Denby to disagree
Nor wealth, fame, mother
to blanket me
Never kisses penetrate
the grieving marrow
"You sleep through the night
    but for this":
sweet widow pills
tiny hexagonal portals
to oblivion

Canzone
for Ted Berrigan, 1934-1983

I crisscross my feelings with a view
of street, people walking, some crazy looking, from a window
Some could be anyone, me, you, Ted, with your own "view"
Could anyone else share? Tinted clouds today. His view
which some thought extreme, distorted, stubborn,
making friends into Myth where they became viewed
with excessive scrutiny & magnified into situations in
     which only the Heavens dare intervene
He said, Propitiate the gods! They love to intervene
as you walk, sleep, talk, make love, drink soda in plain view
of them. I'll put in a good word, you show-offs! I have long talks
with them at night about you, no evasions when the muses talk
This was the energy Ted sought by talk

As if there was no other way close enough to get a multiple view
of self, and tell some history through layers of talk
He would tell his heart to talk
& it did & enlarged the domains of art, his mind was behind a window
out of which he could throw propriety, then remake language,
     steal it from books, from fast elegant talk
to discover the power that lives in printed words & talk
is captive, you can re-invent the world, it's not so stubborn
but tongue-tied, shy, a young girl, gorgeous, funny, also stubborn
about bringing poems into focus. Huddle, team, to talk
Ted lying before his audience in bed, a practiced man, his memory then intervene
fundamental to the thing seen, the thing thought, then Death could intervene

Pugnacious, subversive, president of the adventure, Death intervened
to taste & magnify the ingredients, but also end talk
although I hear it still go on. Mysterious noises intervene
to shake the poet out of her sleep to recognize his cargo, & to intervene
on behalf of Ted who won't ever formulate a neat view
Here is a non-utilitarian cigarette, but it can't intervene
between us anymore, it won't intervene
as you once flicked ash on my lap (I was indignant), then out the window
Or you once beheld all of Boston from my airplane window
Did you ever belong to me? Could I never intervene
to make you healthier, less quivering with stubborn
love or pride? I loved you of course for being stubborn

You were inhabiting the same stubborn
poems as I was. I can't look out the window
without missing you without being angry at you, stubborn
in a kind of grief that won't let me write now, head stubborn
& the typewriter waiting for a new oracle who will talk
vast magical ruminations spelled out from the moment, sing of a stubborn
time insistent upon war for chatter for stubborn stammerings
to make life more exalted, a point of view
which uses dreams because they are my imagination my view
now of you as a full citizen of this country no matter how stubborn
I breathe in the colors from the window
I stand in the early morning light of the window

Are you drawn back to look in my window?
If so, I'll be capacious, I want to ask you something stubborn
"I am a bountiful cotton crop" you wrote on your last postcard window
like a cartoon. Then my name and address: "Mt. Olympus,
     Near Bo-Tree, Manhattan." You draw an octagon window
Your handwriting makes me laugh, it would always intervene
optimistically. Did you mean to keep me in the picture? The window
is shut, I went away, a stranger moved into the apartment,
     no need to shout up at the window

I miss your comparisons, prodigious talk
We are as unlike as people can be in our talk
It is 1967. You call up at the window
with your rotund ambition, a cosmopolitan view
Let's get high, let's fall in love, let's ride uptown & see
      what the painters are doing with a view

Is it nothing more than strange antics, a view
I'll never own, nor you, nor greater intensity than talk
will ever do, when grief does spill over & intervene to the present?
My equilibrium is swaying as the 20th century stubbornly shuts down
I was there & I was there by the window onto you.

Last Dinner

for Edwin Denby, 1903-1983

Evening hot we compliment
Dinner: Katie's cold thick bisque how
Winning & Edwin tells advantage of knowing
Italian well so I'll
Never grow hungry, read for supreme pleasure

Dante & live away from here (his
Eye disturbed by bare bulb, we trade places) He says
Notice how in *Paradiso* love is pure generosity like
Balanchine touch, Dante & Beatrice in *pas de deux*
You can *hear* it in music, *see* language
So too in "Three Poems" He says he never read much but Donne

Engaged in Frank, John, Jimmy later of course but you think
      anything's that good in
Young poets now?
Edwin's sharp eye makes his question claw gratuitously
      like nothing to his
Standard, we'd better get better.

Science Times
("of midnight or moted sunbeam")

Must know all color, must know such tolerance
Must know obsessive wildlife, must cultivate
a heart's content, staring at platform heels,
hennaed hair, must know how to handle with care
all phenomena closing in, a gearshift refuses
to come to life, must know a bedroom & play the
gentle game of love, or live solitary. Something
knows you: the animals, the shrubbery. Must know
the route setting out, must be able to locate by stars
Must be around here somewhere, surf hisses invisibly

Loud noises are the chief attraction to silence
Silence could be grass withering, your own hand,
or beyond restoration, no going back, a silence of toy
asleep during someone's appearance around here,
during anyone's absence too, going out for the news
and coming back, still absent-minded, left a coin or
two hovering over the child, words in a store about it
Words to make up for the silence re-entering now
with a desire to smoke, eat, sleep, read this old book
about desire, how loud it sounds in your ear

Desire, desire, desire, how it sounds in jubilation
The dream can't be sabotaged, it'll sit tight
arms spending a few months around a man
never bolting until one day getting back to work
as if nothing more is necessary, put on your boots,
out you go into dilapidated air, or brisk
fully recovered air the next, happy to stroll
around modern buildings, restored to a living present
not pinched and drawn faces down-at-heels architecture
Where are we going in force in any bright city?

Human fauna of region, river dwellers whose source
is abstract, turning a corner to how conditions get worse
no longer rent stabilized, more building blocks
to urban existence piling up & you think you can't
live inside it anymore, living between a state of mind
& brooding massively over money & air conditions
It seeps in from the river & some say wear a vest
to restrain your excitement, no bad habits
Walk me toward the bridge, toward the memorial,
to Soldiers & Sailors Monument, land & sea nearby, a naked bench

Take up the battle for civilization, in ruins
How death always surrounds you & new ploys for war
Release my commando heart on this purblind delusion
Release any intelligence you, I, we can on whomever
you are talking to, I won't take sides but this
maze of shadowy reasoning like Totalitarianism
something to crash out of, blaze forth from,
know what you're talking about, circle the enemy
with compassion, pity the most evil, cultivate your
bursting heart, free from homespun ropes, these thoughts

cramped, or arguing. Patterns of thoughts running
the same ruts over and over
Purification rituals & within recognizable limits
of course, you just stop that right now, all the
funny stuff, stop your alarming aggression
toward your dinner ware, toward rugs & towels
toward the necessary agenda, toward someone else's
disbelief, stop all tawdry beefing up, war placentas,
Stop lingering over the newspaper, stop mistreating the teller
or the companies that mistreat you, overcharge your account

The doorbell rings it is the taxman, again it is curtains
for the daggerlike slits of windows, rehearse coming and
going so there are no obstacles to imagination, no obstacles
to whatever you see out window: city or suburb or truck or
plane, lights on it's night in this hemisphere, crumpled
road, obscure driving, where to go? Where lovers go, where
men & women & animals lavish praise on the
control of wheel & emotion, getting over the rise in the
road, smile pleasantly in my direction, how far we've
come, look back on quantum mechanics, don't stop

It appears the features of the atomic world become real
only when we look at them with our funny, curious blue &
brown eyes, that they otherwise are in no position to
respond, smeared out over space. They are out there now,
raging around as we do. And we come into focus only
when we look at each other, a little frightened perhaps
separated together or born together in a sense out of the
same human possibility & yet we fly apart at seams
or go away mad. I didn't mean to block your
time. I didn't mean to say that our world would end, how could I?

I meant to be more gentle in the long afternoon,
I meant to never take us out beyond restoration
If what was meant was atavistic I'll take no blame
Comes upon me like animal urge I can't control, you know,
primary colors, scolding the boy wonder. Put aside
off-putting manners, warm up the exchange, uplift the
peasantry: certain mad huts and brains around here
My only hope is self-control with the help of friendly
neighbors, a touch of relief, if there exists any
Such a thing extends the "couple" to the world picture

The Capitalists are not getting enough sleep
Purification rituals for the somber diplomats
risking their lives for the advancement of one way of
thinking. Agreed? The light tumbling from the jet onto
the runway, doors open, rush to the job, or death in some
remote area, she didn't even know the language and
walked into Beirut like a naive child, "Search me,
put up my arms if you like, nothing to hide. I become
more interesting in a foreign tongue, nothing reckoned
beforehand, nothing gained but my distrust & suspicion ..."

Search me & find my gossip and suspicion, search me
for nuts and bolts, search me like the universe,
or search me for neocolonialism, fascism, dandyism
What do you see in these eyes? Search my eyes, search
my mouth for the telltale words, my heart is open
Search my delicate shoes if you will, I'll lie down
while you inspect my corpse, be my guest, all the time
in the world to be a corpse. Is this the scenario?
The boat leaves without you, you will never escape,
a weapon conducts your every move: walk, turn, sign this

Marxism is reduced to caricature in Africa whereas
the Asian is the eternal "other." Happened before: the
mimosa trees ... Happened before with consequences to be
measured: political, social, come this way 'round the branches,
around the petals, step lightly on a spring day
Walking shoes for any country or jungle or blacktop
Safari clothes — lightweight, anonymous, ruling class
and reasonable, or priding itself such, to take tea
at appropriate times, give me some for this unbearable
thirst, wanting the amenities, can you blame the woman?

Blame which is relative to the original mind shining like
a mirror, something like that, image from the old texts
Don't put it aside, consider well before it fades
Consider well, your ingredients, what ticks
beside the heart, beside the clock, the actress in you
Consider what roused in you your infinite sadness
when you saw the day break, finally to go to sleep
or so you hoped & it was a gorgeous day, not a care
about groundwork, or duties with paper, and everyone else
could enjoy it too, freshly washed & breakfasted

Out on the breathing ground for the money, for the heck
of it, putting the car through a wash with those
funny blue brushes. The mops descend like characters
from comics, alien creatures of hemp or fur to smudge
your glass with soap & water, it sure needed it
The flamboyant cost of living demands it too,
dressing beside the motorcar, idling in the roadside dust,
into something more decent. This is a movie set in L.A.
We all saw it together & dreaded the outcome
beach sand, smoking guns, bright lipstick, dread sex

Not that I or anyone does dread sex. Put it another way:
Entry into the person of your desire, that word again
& it is ecstatic, the moment, & then you're here again
the scent of the person beside you bringing you to consciousness
or into sleep, how lovely they are, the lovers
in a sort of droll embrace, touching the edge of the
impossibility of ever holding onto anything again
Do we get it, lapsing into separate thoughts, do we
care to scream in delight at the distance between us,
close & far, you might ask How did we get together?

Who invented it? Desolation & romance. But before you go off
you have another job to do outside there on the pavement
Dress warmly & take an old crate out to the street
Don't get caught in the crossfire, don't cross onto
enemy turf. If you are a Protestant you are enraged
A Catholic wants the right of way, will you never accede?
Contours of the street are sad & worn, a woman weeps at the window
You would wish not to grow up in this old hate, right or wrong
A cerebral battle you might say, chips always down
bloodshed everywhere, stinging pride and dignity in rife street

Economic exploiters everywhere, the Iron Lady among them
She speaks tough, the world gone mad in suffering, who's
listening? A figurehead is speaking figuratively invoking
the wrath of god, we are facing Armageddon & then
it's tasted lethally in methyl isocyanate, its name
lethal, hear it? isolation, cyanide, methedrine, carrying the
sound of death. May this agony haunt the
perpetrators so they wake to action & send attentions
hither to anyone any person any country anywhere in pain
This spell to work free of profit motive's chemical plague

Not meaning to be gruff but I was chilled by this news
& thinking about populations, wild bitterness,
all the scourges and famines: here we are again
colliding in the graveyard. At the same time out of
the sepulcher into the world which is glistening, tender
& animated by joy. Help me into it I say to you, lover,
this address is penned in love,
I tuck myself into an envelope to be a message to myself
as well, roguish glimmer in the eye, nothing but projections
We make the world now we must help the world, go further

Set back the clock on the USS Pittsburgh, take it apart,
dismantle those warheads, dig up the poison & deactivate
its hideousness, admit wrongdoing, & because life is
uncertain, don't seem so arrogant, taking this for granted
You stay out of doors, affirming phenomena perhaps or join
the throng in holiday shopping, exercise tenderness
yet don't tell anybody exactly what to do, create this
atmosphere on a boat, in a train, at the airport in a taxi
Wherever you go you are this living example, how do you do?
How do you find time to manifest all over the place?

In a twinkling hurry, in a bloody hurry, hurrying to meet you,
hurry up the investigation, hurry the obsequious grinners out
of here, hurry to sit down, a welcome interruption,
abstraction enlarges the scope of the canvas so don't hurry
on about that on my account, standing in front of my best
girlfriend's sobriety, enormous cities jammed with humanity
hurrying. I will stop, turn my head in your direction
one last time. Will we ever see each other again?
You pass out of my life, a little steadier, your golden
opportunity down the street, we could never live together

Our heads too strong, you might never let me open
the window yet I'm the one begging for warmth, bad
circulation, reroute these hands, these limbs. Solitude is swell
Your objects had a grip on me, release me I cried, & they did;
oak table, cloisonné lamp, echeveria, statue of Tara. I'm gone,
swept back into other versions of those things, different
sizes and textures, a rehearsal for the next time
How many lamps & beds how many pans & clothes & quilts
& mirrors encircling & filling your space? I wonder
Count them as they disappear, no memory but for the last kiss

in a hotel room in Oregon. Goodbye. Let you go.
I wore a hat to protect my head out of there, showers
of rain breathing more easily accompanying
the heat, & to dream my dream was not my own, given up to
old age, sickness & death
every illusion of persistence destroyed
Shyness does not wear away, but sits like a stranger
in your midst with a sister who resembles nothing more
or less than boldness, the way she dresses, the carriage
of her tall pert body, not yet size 12, coming into her own

So many characters out under the hot sun today,
yesterday too. Many days passed where I walked with you,
you were one of them. But now you are different,
the shy one, & I will take the part of boldness
although I am bigger than the miniature on the canvas
Step out of the frame, out of context & climate
Come alive with a vengeance, you glow with radiance
absorbed in paint, art turns into life finally
and close by is the Museum you turn to, a vampire as day dawns
over raucous city I'll be a still life if you like me this way

Enough of you. You make me crazy and untidy, you make me
feel so young, meaningless etc. You make of me no scientist but
flamboyant and suspicious to the young clerk, you make me
forget politics & passion. Go away, you are a nemesis
of forgetting, you are my past dignity, I give up the ghost
of you. You are an impromptu meal. Ax, you bring out my
atavism, you are a parcel of melancholy, you are gray clouds
massed in the sky overhead, running for cover
You dress like a European to fool me, you are a dunce,
you are shimmery & indistinct in the rain, you are persuasive

But you wouldn't regale me unabated like a country club
The imperialists are not happy nor do they swoon in fear
It's an edge about them, they wear it like a cloak
Deficiency of some kind doesn't explain fear, too much protein
but the cloak might. Hiding like a criminal, uncomfortable
because of all the self-aggrandizing secrets, hush it up,
how creative instinct atrophies, women grab their chance now
to be new faces on the scene, think of a new topic although
I can't quite drop you yet, you who seem to not be there
& won't return my calls, you who remain silent &

pitted against yourself, no my dream can't be sabotaged
It likes the clothing & this foaming at the mouth
What one can do best with words: stop all the killing
& take down your heart on paper, it's a sumptuous occasion,
one in which you could speak out, or shout,
not a bewildered gaze but straight out through the sockets
to rediscover what you already know, what everybody's
been telling you but you were beside yourself. Now you
are here, seeing & speaking, the meandering paths are one
Get on with it, you can do it, you are a technical skill

You are discovering a new planet beyond the solar system
orbiting a distant dim star in the constellation Ophiuchus,
showing that planetary systems are not unique to the sun
although this is not a true planet, perhaps a brown dwarf,
a failed star just as our sun is not a major star but is in
the G-dwarf class. How we denigrate those we worship! The further
away the better, perhaps atrophied, perhaps active. Why hurry?
I foresee the beginnings of a book on the subject
A dream is not fortuitous, inclement weather keeps you in
You are grounded again trying to get to Van Biesbrocck 8B

You can't. I'll help you stay here, you have a stricken look
Soil erosion is a gentler obsession the megalopolitan
can't identify with. He tries & lights his way home, treading
the earth or so he thinks, it feels silken or rough
We are projecting a regenerative pleasant time, salaries increase
in such a cerebral revolution, pure fantasy, something cooked up
to ignore the past. For past is past the people quite agree
not the mausoleum of a long dead Queen, deepening twilight of
this kalpa working its way into your senses, haven of ignorance
The senses could be the ticket to enlightenment if they opened up

A Polish priest is brutally murdered, do they open?
Starvation caused by drought, now flooding in Ethiopia
Do your senses open up? Are you western born or from the east?
Are your parents living? What do they do? Are you an educated
person? Does music excite you? Do you want to change the
world, stop time, die, travel, procreate? What gives? Apartheid?
Are you self-reliant or do you always depend on others for
the next meal, vacant sublet, rides to the country?
Do you miss people when they aren't around? Could you stand to
be really poor? Are you sick, always whining

about your latest injury? Let your psychological contours
be full of grace, not a somber spectacle
Don't hate me either for giving advice, I can't help
it, I am the reporter armed with a tape recorder
I've been watching you many years, you can't hide a thing
but the processes of your work which remain, still,
a mystery, not to paint too dark a picture about you the person
You the artist are okay. Resentment, where does it come from?
The lovers forget to quarrel until one day it spills out
all over the street, onto a fresh napkin, they are so civilized

Ethiopia exists on a high plateau & is fenced by deserts
& sea at the northeastern tip of Africa. The ascent of
the plateau starts at Massawa, Ethiopia's port on the Red Sea
almost at sea level & goes as high as 8 feet above sea level.
Ras Dashan at 15,000 feet is the highest mountain. Crater
lakes like Lake Tana exist. The famed Blue Nile Abbay flows
to Lake Tana. There are many known rivers. The Cataract
Chis-isat (smoke of fire) formed by Abbay is especially
beautiful. Prehistoric sites & documents show complex
migrations of outsiders with light hair, semitic features

Ezana, the great Axumite king accepted the Christian faith
& made it the state religion. But the decline of the Axumite
Empire begun in the 7th Century was followed by the growth
of Muslim power over Arabia & most of North Africa. During
those times of war & unrest Church music assumed its complex
stylistic traits & church leaders attempted to communicate
Igzi-abher, who is the creator of Earth & the Universe, through
music. Church music is a composite of melody, zema, Kine
poetry & aKuaKuam movement. During times of sadness & anger
secular patriotic song style was born to waken hatred of Muslims.

Be that as it may; some history. Is it agreeable that to
every gene it is possible to assign one primary action
& conversely every enzymatically controlled chemical
transformation is under the immediate militaristic supervision
of one gene & one gene only? Then Harris, a protégé of Penrose
used the new technique of paper chromatography to study
the aminoaciduriasis or something like that. You could say it
was successful in finding possible metabolic error, you
could say by naming things you understand them — purvey, pursue,
fall in love with them, free of them then, let them go

although they could haunt you still. Many wise cultures
making predictions for this time a few thousand years
ago were clear on the disordering of our environment
Tell me about it, how can you not "believe" & jump
on the little bandwagon. You will never be a funny person
at this rate, somewhat obsessed by what "the world" is
not doing, and be persistent in harping on what won't be there
except not a homogeneous variety of persons (the baker, the candlestick
maker). You can help them by your research, money, & attentions
If you could but see us all here, toasting you, you'd light up

Send off the packages now so as to avoid the rush or crush
Not a bit like a pneumatic tube I'd thought so fondly of
Whatever became of a bright idea? Who fell asleep on it?
If those people are listening I hope they aren't disappointed
we aren't shouting aren't parading about it, although
it comes up & we could be potential buyers. Death takes
its toll, the saying is something like this, a knell, & is
going to depress someone or other but how can that be deemed
such a terrible thing. Pressure to keep the subject under
wraps or in a hush, & walking away from the conversationalist

nipped any embarrassment in the proverbial bud, but
any proverb would have more stature here. Can you remember
the appropriate one? Nothing repeating in my memory,
nothing treacherous, nothing unrelenting, nothing muffled
or motorized, nothing aspiring exactly, but let it seem
tame, so much illness in winter in this hemisphere,
can't lick it. My point of view is shared by red blood cells,
be they as they may & the symptoms are patriotism,
dualism, realism, insistence, sanitation, blinding rain
& an interest in the scientific field of heredity, I *do* exist

Night light, the little edge, & silhouettes against
the sky of treetops of front range of jagged rock
and let this be a lesson unto you, a solstice of good
cheer, the weather says that wind & bird sounds restore
your senses, also bell-ringing. So that now you have the
gift of speech, of eyes, ears, nose, taste, of smell of
mind, & all the accouterments. You do exist coming out
of a forest of hermae (a strange dream) these talking heads of
bygone men who seek to warn or guide you, don't listen!
Don't listen for they are stone, and give a male slant to history

Stone could be moved by your inestimable tears
the Frog Prince says to the beautiful young woman for
she is convincing in her grief, bereft of a golden plaything
& why should a frog believe a temperamental spoiled thing?
Why should I ever believe you, how could we agree?
Yes, she's a nice woman ..... a long pause, or you could say
Corpses that are active go on like this day after day
but never thinking to offer up their senses
for the benefit of mankind, a grand idea
Let's sit & talk about it, here on this mossy rock

Great big moon the children reach for tonight
We push against each other for a sense of wildness
& the thrill of telling me I don't exist
not wanting to encourage competition or getting
in such a corner nothing could be settled. Sit down
again with more submission, please. Don't leave me
overcrowded wondering what to do next in the dark
People get sententious or harsh, take a choice
as you take a stretch from your advantageous position
When a person is so fond of another it's no secret

You just show the chill of it, apprehension about
keeping a secret, it slips out, no indication of value
now, you assent warily with a nod beneath your tension
How you get a hold of me with your soft touch each time,
certain junctures the woman can't say no to, brooding
for no good reason on trivial matters until lunch is ready
It's the next day! Something critical & homemade is served
up, not without its effect on the spirits of the guests
a whole houseful nimbly awaiting a turn at the sink
all with the appearance of being fairly hypnotized

Then our revelations are told, one by one, stonily
at the table, not pretending to any greater gift of
intelligence but a fear of being positively silly &
wasted like the anarchic confusion in a mob, something
like another meaningless four years of a dangerous presidency
full in the sun, neither relief nor gratification
the actors no longer heroic but futile, rage filling
my co-called soul & then someone drops something
as if the fiber of everyone's being is asleep
As if to say bluntly: Wake up to a new conspiracy!

Not really an answer but a respectable attitude is needed
showing independence, humor, miscellany, precision
& other delicacies of the cushioned angle waiting
to be authorized or trying to cauterize the future with
a point of view, & piqued when it doesn't work out
the way we're all projecting on the common stage which
oscillates in the status of this image. It comes & goes
meting out its own predictions of what happens next
So we're left guessing the odds of something chemically remote
or close by, always thinking the worst & then forgetting

The flicker of a sense of doom which is a disguised
emotion someone is getting off on is not the nature of
responsibility, shifting like light against the table,
new cast of characters now widening the constellation so
that everyone gets a chance to think & speak. This is
a group process thing, hang your coat by the door
You are never as unprepared as you think, a fresh link
to the other Utopians. A group-in-touch can be transforming
until you or your best friend screams Let me out of here!
I'd rather arrange a career in other things

The light changed again & a note of eagerness
was reported in the dailies, the votaries parenthetically
jeered, yet ready for any sacrifice, & let each other
off the hook. It was difficult enough getting married
why clutter up the room housing more mirrors?
People give little lunches & then leave someone else
in the lurch, you can see the body nervously turning
or curling like a question mark, what spot to put
the energy in next? It was all over like a theater piece,
you can all go home now, it's dusk you can still find the way

Imminence of war or want of scheming, a revolt against
despotism we hope, not simply a puppy understanding
Everybody saying a thing does not make it right after all
Even with eloquence you have to rapidly translate
its meaning these days, seize on the significant
which will enable you to see clearly the diagnosed vices
in any situation. Take Nuclear Winter, for example,
although we'd rather not dally with that one, just paint
its terribleness with a few quick strokes, not a lot of
turbulence of imagery, thank you. We are better off

if we know the facts. I've never been able to
convince a multitude. Delight's another animal, a hare or
tortoise? you may ask, it seems to matter these days. These
days: speedy perception's what's needed, although I have a
rueful recollection for the times before the invention of
the telephone because then you might write me long letters
& synchronize our events in a more leisurely way, but
"then" is not "now," although she could be the daughter of —
kind of outdoorsy, wearing britches & descending from
the moors resembling the shadow of someone's scholarly

idea that beckons to you to leave off this nonsense about
the end of civilization. What a harrowing obsession,
an inducement to going back to bed & sleeping it off
although it leaves me without your company, dear comrades
in oblivion, creatures of circumstances, although you may ask
Who created what? Come back into my memory stress & sadness
and let me banish you once & for all & bring back
the convivial parties, the flushes of enthusiasm for books,
ideas, lovers, optimism in the act of tying a shoe. Idolatry
falters & renounces all hopes of ever being

a catchall, but we're glad too, what an unexpected relief
The mystery of a cosmic origin might yet be solved
One of the sources, Cygnus X-3, a two-star system believed
to lie on the outer fringes of the Milky Way, has been found
to produce so many of higher energy cosmic rays that it could
account for the galaxy's entire production. Cygnus X-3 is
assumed to be a pulsar, a fast rotating star of extreme density
that circles & draws gas from a companion star. When high
energy protons strike the atmosphere they generate showers
of secondary particles that reach earth, a most powerful radiation

All the trouble spots & places of confused resolve
are manifesting: Ayacucho for one, Sendero Luminoso
frustrated in an attempt to light the way. What is the
"path" quality to murder or other atrocities? On the other
hand, we must call for an end to the suffering of the "disappeared"
that provoked the Shining Path in the first place & abandon
our torpor. The poem, for all its illusion of impassioned moralistic
speech, a structure of gestures of humanity towards you,
still begs you to hold life sacred & resist oppression as
President Belaunde Terry places 9 western provinces under control

An attack which could be made from another quarter maintains
the balance that could manifest without fake apologies
A tinge of absoluteness about any politics & you
want to remain indoors, rejecting the world in order
to possess it differently, perhaps. Oppositions
always tend to come together, a golden bird & a scarecrow
I wish to learn an exquisite language & put myself at
the mercy of midnight or moted sunbeam, all the rest of
experience falling in between, as a dogged pupil learns the game
Rise & put on your foliage & wake the half-awakened birds

The prevailing atmosphere of a game is noted here
The secrets of a lady's study are noted here
Form & content are inseparable & are noted here while
a cheerful distance is maintained by the esthete
The athlete, on the other hand, jumps in the ring &
faces not an easy problem to solve, blurring out distinctions
as he falls back weak of head. What is noted here is the
incongruity of the word "earth" when it's used as a foil
for "heaven," good little boys & girls or unmannerly
ruffians fighting on the ground, an aggregate for anything

basic that occurs out in the day or night, planet-bound,
disciplined in the tradition of the tragedy of "either/or"
& taking one's pick, so that anyone is suspected
of guerrilla activity in Peru. The Emergency Zone is
filled with hundreds of unidentified bodies, help that
the tears be not idle, address your letters to the ambassador
& the President, life could be more precious than you
realize, don't let the world exist unnaturally
The rhetoric continues, every context is crucial
in this proposition, to encounter the enemy, address these woes

Aspirations & apprehensions are addressed
An imaginative grasp of diverse materials is necessary
to the whole picture, & if the recent study reported
in the daily newspaper is accurate, altruism is something
that could be nurtured, stemming from self-confidence
Honor is not a dry abstraction nor a matter of fact
but approaching the end of any stanza it seems to relate
to the past in this student's mind, this outward show,
only a technique or mannerism perhaps, contemplation
of irony needed in her estimation. Paradox needed

as the case may be in a firmament of time, or as the
case may be in a determined time when the bird is the
same old symbol of freedom, retains its charm
I want to name more creatures in the panorama to
project a sense of wellbeing & joy so that by contrast
suffering is better understood then we stop quibbling
over degrees, who does what to whom, not be interested
in simple "tags." The hermitage of the spirit is in this
precise body, you in yours & suffering whatever blows —
that word again, not to sound condescending I mean

about how language changes but never changes the word
"suffering" to be obsolete, one wishes the blows less
harsh. How a different shade of Rouge will inflict a
different dogma to root out the enemies of the poor, the
real people. What shade are you, not a matter of skin but
of persuasion and style, how are these policies to be trusted,
who at this point could "save" Cambodia? A question to no
one's attention in particular. It is a morass of pain
so acute you deadened your mind to less comprehend the
enormity of genocide. What goes on has gone on before, you

tell yourself, reasoning analytically & then synthesizing
imagination gets the best of you. You scream and beat
your fists in the horror of it, when will time reap its
softening changes,when could any thing or one live in
bliss & emptiness, so to speak, or something palpable
where the scene is reduced & the characters & situations
become manageable at least in our minds, so that the darkest
route is not taken. It makes one less skeptical, less existent
The Elf attacks the evil Pagan, all's not well but
wait, here come more apologies, new evidences, confessions,

reversals, karmic debts, a wild animal's frightful mien,
shades of religion, tapestries, shock, wonder, revenge,
melancholia, inspections, contradictions, resolutions,
idle tears, chill mornings, hand-to-mouth insights.
Is there trepidation too at the sound of a footfall,
someone coming for you, the agents beneath your "soul"?
So to speak: imagination perceives what is outside
So to speak: the outcast lives inside you waiting to
be invited back, night passing on again, no bitterness,
a re-emergence of your old desire, a welcome erotic situation

This is not all, but you are catapulted back into
dailiness, a value both in art & in your job
You are paid to have a kind of mind about something
an analogue perhaps, so that your speech
could correspond to the sound of the many haunting
machines that people your landscape, so many toys for
your fingers & yet you mimic them, calling them
"people" in fact is an indication that they are to
be considered playthings. No one minds that as long
as you & I % she & they know who's boss. Who is boss?

It's code name is Sigma Tau & is far from the laboratory
where lasers are built whose resonators are compact
cylinders instead of long narrow tubes, some day to be
packaged into the smallest volume possible. Also to be
mentioned is "space-fed" radar or array, using a flexible
plastic membrane embedded with many tiny antennas that can
be unfurled like a window shade, or smart projectiles whose
mission is hit to kill, whose miss distance is zero
accelerating on the order of tens of hundreds of
thousands of times greater than the force of gravity

Where does it get us in the long run when time runs
out? I sort of go home and worry at night, admits Walquist
Yet the fire remains unquenched by any apprehension
or rational feelings, getting more inarticulate as the
setup demands us not to be & represents the
split between this earthly warring existence & the
prospect of developing a source of electrical power
for use in space, can't let well enough alone
It is a continual race of arms to see who can hold
out the longest in a kind of insanity. Never let go!

People come in with new thoughts all the time
& their patterning is less obvious. Their curiosity
inspires a cult of stones, a cult of pillars, a cult
of weapons, the cult of trees & animals, cult of
alleys & chapel bells, cult of signs & tokens,
the cult of prodigies, the cult of sobriety, cult of
appliances, cult of talkers, of vast magical ruminations,
the cult of deprivation, the cult of museums & stiff
collars, the cult of perishing in a golden cloud of dust,
the cult of cities, the cult of irony, a cult of madness

Others arrive with a different approach, more mechanized,
whose patterning is equally mysterious, but whose power
is uncontrollable. The supercomputer demands
perfection of vast, elaborate sound-by-sound tracking,
aiming, firing. To do the job, computer software
containing on the order of 10 million instructions
would have to operate flawlessly. I give up! I could
never do it, being ineptly human. Everything balks inside
about this nightmare of technology & yet I
wish to understand the most complex systems

so as to meet the devil face to face, some kind of
prenatal recollection of a snake-haired gorgon,
or the child's eye which sees the divine or is divine
in its relation to the scaffoldings of a multifarious
"system." Don't give up, don't leave the lover cloyed
& panting, retain your moisture & heat, be an organic
thing with neuronic turnover like the handsome canaries
whose parts of the brain which control song structure
have to relearn those notes again & again each spring
reminding the heart regeneratively to sing.

Said So

They said must not, must not be said. They said it:
must not be said. Must not must not must not be said.
They settled it, way leading to a future, lately acquired,
way leading to a future tense. Must not. Said so. Said
not. Will not. I said I am throwing the words. I said
I am throwing the words around. I said something is forming.
Something is forming

    I said I am throwing the words around something is forming.

        (make it to me to me to me to heal me up again
          make it to me to me to me to heal it up again)

Said: I am spilling the words around.

Tell sky I'm coming
Tell sky I'm coming

They are this old world getting busy with trouble now
They are getting busy with trouble this world

Now heal it up again

        (make it to me to me to heal me up again)

I said I am throwing the words around something is forming.

Will be. Said will be will be said. Said it now: will be
said. Said so. Something is forming.

        (make it to me to me to me to me to heal again)